Mysterious

of Dorset

by Robert Westwood

ISNBN 978-0-9552061-5-3
© Robert Westwood 2007

Inspiring Places Publishing
2 Down Lodge Close
Alderholt
Fordingbridge
SP63JA

www.inspiringplaces.co.uk

Above: The avenue
of beech trees near
Badbury Rings.

Front cover: Durdle Door
Rear cover: Athelhampton House

Printed by ACH Colour, Bournemouth

1

Contents:

Acknowledgements:

Thanks to my wife "Steve" and to Mandy and Alan for all their help and support.

Other titles by *Inspiring Places Publishing:*

Fossils and Rocks of the Jurassic Coast
Ancient Dorset
Day Tours in the East of Dorset
Dark Age Dorset
Smugglers' Dorset
Alien Big Cats of Dorset

Check out the photo gallery and buy books and prints online at:

www.inspiringplaces.co.uk

Introduction

Dorset is a county rich in legends and folklore. Celts, Romans, Anglo-Saxons, Vikings and Normans have all left their mark on the county. For centuries people have worked the land and the sea around its beautiful coastline. Perhaps, in the past, Dorset's people understood the land and natural elements far better than most do in our modern age but it is not surprising that myths and legends have grown up around things that were not understood.

With the signs of ancient civilisations scattered all over the county it is natural that barrows, standing stones and stone circles would be associated with strange happenings. Also natural that, given the violent clashes with invading armies, in times of civil war and between smugglers and the Law, that tales of all manner of spectral apparitions would be passed down the generations.

Interesting as this folklore is, the real and verifiable history of Dorset is equally fascinating. Luckily, for the interested visitor, there are many beautiful locations in the county where history and legend intertwine to provide a wonderful story. This book picks out such places.

Above: Eggardon Hill, an Iron Age hillfort near Bridport, is associated with all kinds of paranormal activity.

Eastbury House, Tarrant Gunville [5 miles NE of Blandford]

Sitting in the quiet village of Tarrant Gunville, the remains of Eastbury House provide a perfect setting for tales of the supernatural. The village is one of relatively few in Dorset whose name derives from the Celtic era; the word "tarrant" comes from a Celtic word meaning "trespasser", referring to the little Tarrant stream which frequently spills over its channel in winter months. The house itself was once one of the largest and grandest in all England, built by a man with fabulous wealth and a colourful reputation. Add to this mix a wicked steward and a tale of deceit and we have a true story to match the legend that has grown up around it.

In 1718 George Doddington, Lord of the Admiralty, commissioned the great architect John Vanbrugh to build him a house that would rival Blenheim and Castle Howard. Doddington died in 1720 and left his estate to his nephew George Bubb. Bubb-Doddington was determined to finish the project and by 1738 was the proud owner of a magnificent stately home which had cost around £140 000, a huge amount in those days. By all accounts he was a vain man, overweight and possessed by a desire to achieve positions of ever greater importance. He was a member of parliament for several constituencies and eventually rose to be Treasurer to the Navy and was raised to the peerage in 1761. Bubb-Doddington was also a member of the infamous Hellfire Club, known more formally as the "The Friars of St. Francis of Wycombe". What the members got up to is still debated but tales of satanic orgies may have been somewhat exaggerated.

When George Bubb-Doddington died in 1782 the house was sold to Richard, Earl Temple and on his death passed to his son George, the second Earl Temple. It is around this time that our ghostly story begins. The first earl had found the house too big and expensive to maintain and the second earl even tried to pay someone to live in and look after the place. When he was forced to live in Italy for health reasons he decided to take drastic action and have most of the house demolished.

This is where the wicked steward enters the story! William Doggett had been employed by Earl Temple to look after his affairs while he was away and was charged with arranging for parts of the house to be demolished. It seems Doggett didn't follow his master's instructions very closely and pocketed the money received from the sale of building stone. Doubtless Doggett never expected the earl to return again and when told that he was on his way, realised that he would be unable to conceal his wrongdoings. He went into the house and shot himself.

On some nights, it is said, a coach with a headless horseman arrives at Eastbury carrying Doggett who enters the house and re-enacts his suicide. The story does not end here; Doggett was buried in the nearby church of Tarrant Gunville and when this was being rebuilt in 1845 his coffin was dug up and his body found not to have decayed. His legs were bound with a yellow ribbon. The villagers assumed Doggett was one of the "undead", a vampire!

Above: The decayed main entrance to the once magnificent Eastbury House where the phantom coach with the headless horseman is said to appear.

Cerne Abbas [8 miles north of Dorchester]

No village in Dorset is better equipped to fire the imagination of a visitor than Cerne Abbas. As you enter the village from the main Dorchester to Sherborne road you will see the main reason many people visit Cerne Abbas, the Cerne Giant. This 180 feet high figure carved in the chalk hillside remains an enigma to this day. Experts are still not decided whether he is an ancient carving or a more recent effigy carved as a practical joke. There is no record of him before 1694 and some think he may represent a historical figure such as Oliver Cromwell. Others believe he is far more ancient and may be a representation of the god Hercules.

A famously provocative figure such as this is inevitably going to have legends associated with it and the giant does not disappoint! One tradition tells how a giant once feasted on nearby sheep then lay down to sleep on the hillside where he was killed by the local villagers. They traced his figure in the turf to commemorate the event. He has long been associated with superstitions involving fertility, it being said that to cure infertility a woman must sit on the figure of the giant. Others have said that more intimate action is required to fully utilise the charm; this may be why General Pitt-Rivers, in his capacity as Director of Public Monuments, decided to enclose the figure!

If you stop to look at the giant you will probably be joined by many other tourists, but go a few hundred yards and you may have an even more mysterious and sacred spot all to yourself. Cerne Abbas grew up around the Benedictine monastery founded in AD 987. Legend associates this area with St. Augustine and in particular the Silver Well, sometimes called St. Augustine's Well. It is to be found in the corner of a churchyard close to the meagre yet beautiful remains of the monastery. There are a number of versions of the story involving Augustine being abused or conversely impressed by the propriety of locals; but all have him subsequently striking the ground with his staff and causing a spring to issue forth.

A more probable and appealing legend is that it was the site of a hermitage occupied by St. Edwold, a member of the royal family of Mercia, in the 7th century who set off in search of it following a vision. When he came to Cerne Abbas he gave silver pennies to shepherds in return for food and water. They brought him to the well.

A lovely superstition associated with the well is that it is beneficial to dip new born babies in it as the first rays of the sun touch the water. It is a lovely, peaceful spot, ideal for quiet reflection.

Above: St. Augustine's Well or the Silver Well at Cerne Abbas. Below left: The gateway to the Abbot's Porch, part of the remains of Cerne Abbey.

Right: The Hospice at Cerne Abbey Below right: The village sits beneath the famous giant.

7

Above: Ruined coastguard cottages look over Worbarrow Bay. In the 19th century the Coastguard Service was formed to combat the smuggling trade; only later did it undertake rescue services. The Iron Age hillfort of Flowers Barrow sits precariously on the cliff top at the end of the bay.

8

Worbarrow Bay [about 6 miles west of Wareham]

Spectacular Worbarrow Bay is reached via a gentle walk from the ghost village of Tyneham. Carved out of soft sands and muds between the more resistant Chalk and the Portland and Purbeck limestones it is one of Dorset's hidden gems. Tyneham was requisitioned by the army in 1943 and is now a beautiful monument to a lost rural way of life.

In the 18th and early 19th centuries Tyneham was a hotbed of smuggling activity, as was almost every village along the coast. Worbarrow Bay was a perfect place to land contraband, isolated, sheltered and with deep water so that ships could anchor just yards offshore. Following the successful conclusion of the war against Napoleon the government had surplus manpower and decided to use it to finally end the hugely damaging smuggling trade. Many ex-navy personnel joined the newly formed Coastguard Service; not a search and rescue organisation as it is today but one formed solely to combat the illegal traders. The ruined cottages you see near the beach at Worbarrow were the homes of members of the local coastguard. The 1851 census records 37 households in the parish of Tyneham; the heads of 10 of these were in the Coastguard Service. Clearly a major effort was being made to stop smuggling and it is fascinating to think how the local community functioned with so many people involved in the "trade" and so many of the "other side" in their midst!

One ghostly legend about Worbarrow concerns the contest between smugglers and the Revenue officers whose job it was to oppose them. One night a lone smuggler was spotted by a party of Revenue men. He foolishly fled along the beach where the chalk cliffs are sheer and impossible to climb. In desperation he ran into the sea and was ruthlessly stoned to death by his pursuers. On dark nights his screams can sometimes still be heard mingling with the endless crashing of the waves and a ghostly figure is occasionally seen thrashing in the surf.

Another legend is on an altogether grander scale. On the chalk cliffs above Worbarrow Bay are the precipitous remains of Flowers Barrow, an Iron Age hillfort now half disappeared with the crumbling rock. There is a beautiful walk along the ridge with spectacular views over the Isle of Purbeck. It was on this ridge on a December night in 1678 that the master of the local manor, along with many of his workers, saw and heard what they thought was an army marching. They must have been sure because several hundred soldiers were readied at nearby Wareham. The story was first related by the Rev. Hutchins writing his *History of Dorset* in 1774. He tells how the master, Captain Laurence, was called to London to explain. Since then others have claimed to have seen the phantom army or heard and felt strange things on dark winter nights. Who could they have been? Perhaps war weary Romans marching away from yet another slaughter of ancient Britons?

Knowlton Church [7 miles north of Wimborne]

Knowlton is one of the most special places in all of Dorset. In his book *Ancient Stones of Dorset*, Peter Knight says that "Knowlton is a very sacred geomantic site with many strands of earth mysteries woven into its landscape". Briefly, Knowlton is a Neolithic henge monument with the ruins of a medieval church inside. It was, of course, not uncommon for churches to be built on what were originally pagan sites. Interestingly, the church at Knowlton may have been built using the standing stones that once formed part of the original complex. Research has confirmed that Knowlton was indeed a complex and, in the late Neolithic and early Bronze Age, a ceremonial centre perhaps ranking in importance with Stonehenge.

The church was built in the 12th century and Knowlton was a thriving village well into the 15th century. The circle was formerly used as a meeting place for the local Saxon Hundred and its annual fair became very well-known. In the 15th century Knowlton suffered the fate of many small villages when it was decimated by the Black Death, although the church continued to be used right up until the 18th century.

No surprise, considering its history, that Knowlton is regarded by many as a strange and somewhat magical place. Drive past on a late, sunny, summer's evening and you will usually see someone soaking up the atmosphere. Local dowsing experts also regard Knowlton as something special and much work has been done here by the Wessex Dowsers. It is claimed that, using their techniques, they were responsible, in 2005, for finding an ancient stone from the henge.

Given all this magic and mysticism it is perhaps surprising that Knowlton's legend is a rather mundane affair by comparison, involving the disappearance of the church bell.

As recounted by JS Udal in his book *Dorsetshire Folk-lore* it appears that many years ago the church had a particularly valuable bell. It attracted the attention of thieves who planned to steal it and sell it, perhaps across the Channel in France. Although a remote position, a church bell is a difficult thing to conceal and the band were discovered and pursued. They got as far as the neighbouring village of Sturminster Marshall when they realised they would not be able to escape. They threw the bell over a bridge into the River Stour. The people of Knowlton tried to retrieve it with ropes but no matter how many times they tried, at the last minute the ropes broke. In another version of the legend it is the thieves themselves who go back for the bell but are unable to pull it up; giving rise to the folk song:

Knowlton Bell is stole
And thrown into White Mill Hole
Where all the devils in hell
Could never pull up the Knowlton Bell.

Above: Knowlton Church sitting inside a Neolithic henge. It is easy to see why it is regarded by some as a sacred spot. The clump of trees to the left of the church is the Great Barrow, the largest round burial barrow in Dorset.
Below: Whitemill Bridge, from where the Knowlton Bell was dropped.

Badbury Rings [on B3082 north-west of Wimborne]

Badbury Rings dominates the local landscape. Approach it through the famous avenue of beech trees [the B3082 north-west of Wimborne] and you will glimpse it on the northern side, its summit now densely wooded. Badbury is one of Dorset's many hillforts, built in the Iron Age by the Durotriges tribe and probably one of the twenty such forts that fell to the Roman legion commanded by Vespasian following the invasion of 43 AD.

It was clearly a place of some significance in ancient times; three large Bronze Age round barrows are situated below the hill on the west side and two important Roman roads intersect just north of the hill. Many people think it continued to be an important place following the Roman conquest and that a defining moment in British history might have happened there. No wonder a wealth of legends has grown up around Badbury.

Historians are agreed that at the beginning of the 6th century the Saxon advance was temporarily halted by a British victory at the Battle of Mount Badon. According to some sources the British leader at the battle was Arthur. More reliable sources, however, fail to mention him. Many scholars favour Bath as the likely site of this epic battle, arguing that a study of the names links Bath to *Bathon or Baddon* in Welsh and that it is in a likely position as the East Saxons pushed on towards the west country. Nevertheless there are still some who favour Badbury Rings as the location.

Badbury was, after all, a nodal point in the Roman road system; the Saxons were foot soldiers and it is likely that they would have made use of the Roman roads to move across country. Badbury was on the edge of a great heathland which stretched from Southampton Water to Poole Harbour; the gateway to rich agricultural land beyond. It is a likely point for the Britons to have met the advancing Saxons.

Whatever the truth, a number of legends have grown up around Badbury. Chief amongst these is that King Arthur and his ghostly knights haunt the ancient battleground. It is said that at midnight the sound of battle can sometimes be heard. The "Dark Dorset" website records that in 1970 a group of students camped overnight on the hillfort. In the middle of the night they were abruptly awoken by the sound of clashing metal and shouting: they fled in terror!

Another legend tells us that after his death Arthur took the form of a raven and lives on at the site of his greatest victory. In addition to all this the "Paranormal Database" tells us that other sightings have included a ghostly warrior on horseback, the ghost of a woman in a black dress and an ugly dwarf-like creature that peers into parked cars. Clearly, for those of a nervous disposition, Badbury Rings is not the place to be on a dark, windy night!

Ashmore [5 miles south-east of Shaftesbury]

Sitting in an isolated corner of Cranborne Chase, Ashmore is reputedly the highest village in Dorset at around 700 feet above sea level. Standing on chalk, it is surprising to find a village pond that never seems to dry up. It is lined with clay and may have been developed in Roman times. The Roman road from Badbury to Bath passes close by the village and a number of burial barrows testify to the ancient origins of this settlement.

It seems a peaceful place now but in the 18th century, Ashmore and other villages of Cranborne Chase were anything but peaceful. Deer, protected by law for aristocratic hunters, were the cause of bloody encounters between gamekeepers and poachers. Villagers struggled to protect their crops from the deer, yet there were harsh punishments for those harming them. Many smuggling routes criss-crossed the wild Chase, leading from the Dorset coast to the market towns inland.

It was a small but thriving community in Saxon times; Domesday records 10 villagers and 6 smallholders. It is not much bigger today; essentially still a cluster of cottages around the village pond, but even so it has its share of local legends.

One such legend is attached to the site of a former burial barrow. The barrow, at Washers Pit on the minor road to the west of the village, is now gone, flattened to make way for a metalled road in 1840. Before that locals would report the mysterious sound of "gabbygammies", weird spirits that made equally weird noises. The ghostly sounds ended when the barrow was levelled to make the road. The remains from the barrow were buried in the village churchyard; perhaps the spirits are now at rest?

There is another ghost story associated with Washers Pit, that of a spectral white lady said to haunt the well. The story goes that one night the cook from the nearby big house had a prophetic dream about the well. She rode out and found a lady, dressed in white, hanging from an ash tree over the well.

Left: The village pond at Ashmore on the northern edge of Cranborne Chase.

Studland [just north of Swanage]

These days Studland is a gentle, peaceful place; a favourite spot for a day out on the beach. Look at its geography however, and it is easy to see why this has not always been so. Cut off from the busy urban area of Poole by the entrance to the great harbour, bounded on the south by the chalk ridge and to the west by the wild expanse of Studland Heath, it feels somehow different and has an exciting and colourful history.

In the 17th century it was an ideal base for pirates. Unable to use Poole Harbour because the narrow entrance would make swift escape impossible, Studland has a gently shelving sandy beach and waters sheltered by the chalk promontory. These same features proved invaluable to smugglers a century or so later, while the heathland aided dispersal of the contraband. No doubt the old cottages and pubs of Studland could tell many tales of adventure and intrigue.

A number of legends have grown up in and around Studland. Perhaps the silliest is that the Agglestone, a great natural ironstone boulder on the heath, was thrown there by the Devil from the Isle of Wight, apparently aiming for Corfe Castle. Another legend concerns the murder of a smuggler in a cottage. Thereafter the cottage appeared to be in flames when viewed from on board ship; potentially a very useful marker to smugglers' luggers!

Then there is the rather charming story of the ghost donkey whose master was murdered on the heath shortly before Christmas sometime in the 18th century. The donkey, who is white, has appeared to several people on the anniversary of his master's death, sadly roaming the heath.

Above: The ever popular beach at Studland, previously with smugglers, now with holidaymakers!

15

Sherborne's Castles

Set in beautiful parkland on the edge of the ancient town of Sherborne, the two castles there have been part of momentous episodes in English history. They have been owned by great and powerful figures, and the old castle has also featured in the fighting of two civil wars.

Old Sherborne Castle was built in the 12th century for Roger of Caen, Bishop of Salisbury. Roger was a priest of humble beginnings in France who rose to great power after winning the confidence of Henry I. He became the king's chancellor and accumulated vast wealth. After Henry's death Roger at first supported King Stephen in his dispute over the succession with the Empress Matilda. They soon fell out however and Sherborne was besieged and taken by the king's forces. It was then that some say a curse that had been uttered by the great Osmund, first Bishop of Salisbury, began to take effect. Osmund had prophesied doom and disaster to any layman who held land belonging to the bishopric. After Stephen's death the castle was held by the Montagues who, it is said, all suffered misfortune while in possession of the castle. Edward III gave the castle back to the church and for a while the curse was dormant.

Sherborne returned to secular hands during the reign of the child king, Edward VI. He gave it to his chief minister, Edward Seymour, Duke of Somerset. These were troubled times and Somerset's political manoeuvrings eventually led him to the Tower; he was beheaded in September 1552. Had the curse struck again? It was not long before Sherborne fell into the hands of its most famous custodian, the great Elizabethan adventurer Walter Raleigh. Raleigh had reputedly fallen in love with Sherborne after seeing it on his way down to Plymouth from London. He persuaded Elizabeth I to grant him the lease and after finding the old castle uninhabitable, had the new castle or lodge built. Raleigh lived in Sherborne for about 10 years, following a spell in the tower of London. Unfortunately for him, a disastrous expedition to Guiana resulted in fresh claims of treason and Raleigh too met the executioner's axe at the Tower of London.

Was this again the result of the curse or mere coincidence? It is perhaps not surprising that, given the turbulent political situation at the time and the high profile of Somerset and Raleigh, both adventurous and ambitious men, that they should have ended up where they did!

The mystery does not end here however. The "new" castle at Sherborne is one of Dorset's foremost haunted sites, with the celebrated adventurer as the chief spectre! Raleigh's ghost is said to wander the gardens on St. Michael's eve, September 29th. Some say he sits under a tree in the grounds.

Further ghostly encounters have been reported in the castle itself. Peter Underwood in his book *Ghosts of Dorset* tells how some have heard ghostly noises in the castle such as the sound of galloping horses and fighting. He also tells of one lady who witnessed ghostly figures shouting, running and using firearms.

Top: "New" Sherborne Castle owned by the Digby family since 1617.
Above: The old castle can just be seen across the lake designed by Capability Brown.
Right: A view from the castle grounds.

The Vale of Blackmore [the vale to the north and west of Shaftesbury]

The Vale of Blackmore is one of Dorset's richest farming regions. In his novel *Tess of the D'Urbervilles* Thomas Hardy described the vale as it appears from the chalk uplands near Bulbarrow:

"Here, in the valley, the world seems to be constructed upon a smaller and more delicate scale; the fields are mere paddocks, so reduced that from this height their hedgerows appear a network of dark green threads overspreading the paler green of the grass..... Arable lands are few and limited; with but slight exceptions the prospect is a broad rich mass of grass and trees, mantling minor hills and dales within the major. Such is the Vale of Blackmoor."

From various places on the chalk escarpment there are equally glorious views of the vale, that from the walk alongside the ancient abbey in Shaftesbury springs particularly to mind. To some, from such a viewpoint, the cultivated fields and woodlands must seem like a promised land.

In days gone by this was a rich hunting ground frequented by royalty. It is from this activity that a lovely, if rather sad, legend emanates. It appears that King Henry III was hunting in the vale one day near the village of Holwell. After a particularly strenuous chase the king found his exhausted quarry was a beautiful white hart. The king respected the proud beast and let him go. Sometime later a local gentleman and keen huntsman, Sir Thomas de la Linde, caught and killed the animal. Legend says that de la Linde had coveted the beast for some time and had heard of the king's encounter with him. We do not know if he failed to anticipate that the king might be angry when he heard of the hart's fate or if he merely did not believe the story. Whatever his thoughts, he had made a grave mistake. De la Linde was imprisoned and heavily fined. What is more, from that day on, the owners of his estate were required to pay a yearly tax to the king known as "White Hart Silver".

JS Udal in his book *Dorsetshire Folk-lore* tells how he tried to trace the records of this payment without much success. Mysteriously though, he found that "White Hart Silver" was being paid in the reign of Henry VIII by an estate in another part of Dorset. He also found a strong oral tradition from descendants of the owners of the estate that the tax was real.

Further legends grew up around the white hart itself. It is said that the animal was a magical creature that had survived for centuries in the woods of the area. When it was killed by de la Linde, stabbed in the waters of the River Lydden, a golden collar was round its neck. On it were ancient words, which today can be seen on the sign which stands on a small green in the village of King's Stag.

Right: The sign on the green in the village of King's Stag recalls the words found on the collar of the white hart.
"When Julius Caesar Landed Here, I Was Then A Little Deer.
When Julius Caesar Reigned King Round My Neck He Put This Ring.
Whosoe'er Shall Me O'ertake, Spare My Life For Caesar's Sake."

Below: The rich farmland of the Vale of Blackmore seen from Bulbarrow Hill, one of Thomas Hardy's favourite spots.

19

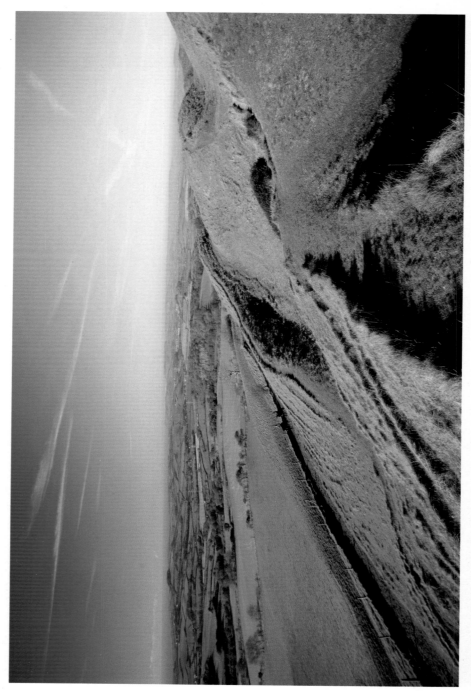

The Iron Age hillfort of Eggardon Hill

Eggardon Hill [5 miles north of Bridport]

Eggardon Hill near the peaceful village of Powerstock is a spectacular place steeped in history and bristling with legends. Another of Dorset's Iron Age hillforts, like Maiden Castle it is one of the more impressive. Massive banks and ditches enclose nearly 40 acres. Bronze Age burial barrows indicate that this is another site long regarded as special. It may or may not have seen a bitter conflict during the Roman invasion, previous massacres at places like Maiden Castle and Spetisbury might have led to swift capitulations by the Britons further west.

The views from the top are impressive, particularly from the south side where, on a fine day, the coast is clearly visible. It was this view that prompted the hugely successful smuggler, Isaac Gulliver, to purchase Eggardon in the early 19th century. It made a perfect spot for his lookouts to signal to the smugglers' luggers offshore! The roads around Eggardon are narrow and little used but the paths over the top and around the southern ramparts are popular with dog walkers and horse riders. Splendid excursions on a nice summer's day but you wouldn't want to hang about if the sun was setting on a chill December evening.

JS Udal in his *Dorsetshire Folk-lore* has a section on old Dorset sayings; one entry is the rather uninspiring "as old as Eggardon Hill", but it does serve to indicate, perhaps, how venerated this site is by local inhabitants; no wonder legends have grown up around it. Chief amongst these is that Diana, Goddess of the Moon haunts the hill, together with an assorted collection of demons, witches and fairies, collecting souls of the dead. Rodney Legg mentions this in his *Mysterious Dorset* as does the "Dark Dorset" website. Udal makes no mention of it however and I have not found any other sources.

A number of strange happenings have been reported over the years on and around Eggardon. As Rodney Legg details, horses have appeared terrified for no apparent reason, motorists driving past have had their engines die and their watches stop for a while. These things have been reported in local papers as was the case in 1972 of a man whose two dogs were terrified at Eggardon on a routine walk. This happened three nights running, again for no discernible reason, although returning to the spot on three consecutive nights adds little to any supernatural explanation - no wonder the poor dogs were terrified being taken back, and then again!

A version of the "lost souls" story is told by Edward Waring in his *Ghosts and Legends of the Dorset Countryside*. It concerns a farmer, out on the hill late one night, who heard baying hounds and saw a man being chased by hounds and a strange dark figure with sparks coming out of his boots. He concluded it must have been the devil chasing and tormenting a soul from the dead. Why he should make such a conclusion isn't stated!

Lyme Regis

Lyme Regis is a quaint and popular seaside town with a colourful history. As recently as 1780 it was a larger port than Liverpool. It began when the Saxon king Cynewulf gave land along the River Lym to the monks of Sherborne with a licence to make salt. It was granted its royal charter by Edward I in 1284 and its famous Cobb was first mentioned during the reign of Edward III.

As befits an ancient port, Lyme Regis has its fair share of ghost stories and legends. One is linked to a famous episode in the town's past, the Monmouth rebellion of 1685 and concerns one of history's most reviled villains, Judge Jeffreys, the "Hanging Judge".

James, Duke of Monmouth was an illegitimate son of Charles II. Claiming to be the rightful king he landed with a small force on the beach at Lyme Regis in June 1685. The rebellion was quickly crushed. Twelve men who had supported Monmouth were brought back to the town to be hung, drawn and quartered on the beach where the rebellion began. The infamous Jeffreys, who had presided over the subsequent trials, liked to witness the executions and stayed at the Great House [now Chatham House] in Broad Street.

It is here that Jeffreys is said to haunt; he has been seen wearing his robes, wig and carrying a bloody bone. In recent times a number of people have claimed to have heard heavy, ghostly footsteps, presumed to be those of the "Hanging Judge". Many will no doubt hope that this is not a spirit at peace, but one tormented by his evil deeds.

Another well-known spectre of Lyme Regis is the Black Dog. The tale is recounted in a book by Miss Leathes in 1882 and tells how a farmer would return home each night from his labours, settle himself down in one of the two seats by the fireplace and be joined in the other by a mysterious black dog. This went on for months and the farmer got quite used to the beast. However, neighbours urged him to get rid of the dog, and after a night of heavy drinking the farmer, not wanting to look weak, rushed at the dog with a stick. The dog raced upstairs and leapt towards the ceiling where he promptly disappeared. The farmer struck at the ceiling with his stick but there was no hole. A small box fell to the floor which was found to contain a large number of gold and silver coins from the reign of Charles I. The dog was not seen again in the house but legend has it that he continues to haunt the lane outside at midnight.

Above: Monmouth Beach, Lyme Regis, looking towards the town. This is where the Duke of Monmouth landed at the start of his rebellion in 1685 and where some of his supporters were brought to be hung, drawn and quartered.

*Top: Portland Bill lighthouse seen from some of the old quarry workings.
Bottom: Looking over Chesil Bank from the Isle of Portland; not difficult
to see why the inhabitants of Portland have always regarded themselves as
separate from the rest of Dorset.*

Portland

The people of Dorset have long regarded the Isle of Portland as unique and different from the rest of the county. JS Udal, writing in 1922, says that the inhabitants of Portland, "say that they are Phoenicians, have never, until lately, allowed any English, or 'foreigners', as they term us, to hold land in their territory, but have kept themselves a distinct people". Thomas Hardy recognised this difference and called Portland the "Isle of Slingers", a reference to the fact that the ancient Britons used pebbles from Chesil Beach as ammunition for their slings.

Today Portland still feels different, its history of industry, in particular the stone quarrying, contrasts starkly with neighbouring Weymouth, the archetypal seaside resort. Surrounded by an often treacherous sea, no wonder Portland has its fair share of supernatural stories.

A legend that Portland has in common with Lyme Regis is the appearance of a spectral black dog. Apparitions of black dogs are well known throughout Britain and some other parts of the world. The term is now used as a classification of a certain type of ghostly phenomenon, usually, but not necessarily, a black dog. They are sometimes associated with certain places, particularly junctions, pathways and bridges.

Perhaps surprisingly, many of these apparitions are friendly, possibly giving warning of some future trouble. Some are savage however and, fittingly, given its supposed location on the Isle's wild seashore, Portland's black dog is a vicious creature. It lives in a cave near to the Portland Bill lighthouse and lies in wait for an unsuspecting passer-by who it seizes and drags away to a violent, watery death.

Portland has another monster legend, this time that of a sea monster called the Veasta. This creature apparently has the tail of a fish and the head of a giant sea-horse. The Weymouth and Portland Borough Council's web site has details of this, claiming it was first sighted in 1457, again in 1757 by the famous Dorset historian Rev. John Hutchins and several times in living memory, including 1995. One of the sightings was at Church Ope Cove where it was represented as a mermaid by a disbelieving press! Strangely, the legend is not mentioned by the great collector of Dorset folklore, JS Udal and other references to it are difficult to find. Perhaps the legends have got a little confused; Udal does mention a story that in 1457 [coincidentally?] a cockerel was seen rising from the water "having a great crest on its head, a great red beard, and legs half a yard long". He seems to have crowed three times and then disappeared.

Perhaps Udal's cockerel and the Veasta are one and the same; it is odd that sightings of a sea monster, one by a respected academic, have not led to a legend that is more well-known. One would have thought that, with the right sort of publicity, a Loch Ness type industry could have been developed!

Batcombe and Melbury Bubb [11 miles north of Dorchester]

Numerous small villages lie tucked between the spurs of the north Dorset chalk downs. Such farming communities where hardy shepherds have tended their flocks in all weathers on the wild hillsides have typically spawned mystical folk tales and this part of Dorset is no exception. Thomas Hardy chose locations around here to feature in his tragic masterpiece *Tess of the D'Urbervilles*, and incorporated some of the local legends in the story.

Next to the road that runs across the top of Batcombe Hill towards Minterne Magna is a stone pillar known as the "Cross in Hand". Many think the stone may originate from a Roman pillar and its purpose is uncertain; it may have been a simple boundary marker, but there are a number of legends associated with it. Probably the most well-known is the explanation of the stone as marking the site of a miracle.

One cold, stormy night back in medieval times the village priest was called to attend a shepherd on the downs who had been taken ill and was close to death. The priest gathered himself together, remembering to take with him the Holy Sacrament in a little silver box or pyx. When he reached the dying man to his horror he discovered that he had dropped the pyx on the way. Unable to properly deliver the last rites without the Sacrament, he set off to retrace his steps. He must have had little hope of finding it but suddenly the rain stopped and before him he saw a shaft of light hitting the ground. Going towards it he saw, illuminated, the silver pyx. Around the scene cattle and wild animals were gathered staring silently at the miracle. The priest gratefully recovered the pyx and delivered the last rites. To commemorate the event he had the stone erected.

The story is recounted in the poem "The Lost Pyx" by Thomas Hardy. Strangely, in *Tess of the D'Urbervilles* Hardy gives another legend attached to the stone, one that explains its name. The pillar reputedly has the imprint of a hand on its top. In the novel Alec D'Urberville asks Tess to put her hand on the top of the stone and swear she will not tempt him with her charms. He claims the stone is holy but an old shepherd later explains to Tess the true origin of it.

"Cross - no; 'twer not a cross. 'Tis a thing of ill-omen miss. It was put up in wuld times by the relations of a malefactor who was tortured there by nailing his hand to a post, and afterwards hung. The bones lie underneath. They say he sold his soul to the devil, and that he walks at times."

The devil appears again in an elaboration of the pyx legend. It is said that the animals around the apparition are kneeling before it on both knees, except a black horse which only kneels on one. The priest asks the horse who he is and the horse replies that he is the devil, going on to explain that he takes the form of a horse so that men will steal him, get hung and thus surrender their souls!

Left: The churchyard at Melbury Bubb. In the background is Bubdown Hill where Thomas Baker was murdered. [see following page]

Below left and right: The Cross in Hand stone near Batcombe. A number of legends surround this stone and some say there is an imprint of a hand on the top of it. Make your own mind up - the photograph has not been manipulated.

"Some say the spot is banned; that the pillar Cross-and-Hand
　　　Attests to a deed of hell;
But of else than of bale is the mystic tale
　　　That ancient Vale-folk tell. "
[The first verse of "The Lost Pyx" by Thomas Hardy]

A short distance north-west of Batcombe lies the charmingly named Melbury Bubb, a tiny, picturesque village clinging to the foot of Bubdown Hill. Here, real-life macabre events have given rise to a ghostly legend.

In the graveyard of the village church is a tombstone dedicated to Thomas Baker. Its brief epitaph recounts how he was "barbarously murdered" as he led his horse and cart over Bubdown Hill in 1694. Thomas was a local merchant and had been returning from the neighbouring village of Evershot. There were no witnesses to the crime on the isolated track and for seven years the perpetrators went unpunished. They might have escaped for ever if they had not been overheard arguing about the crime in a local pub. They were swiftly arrested, tried and sentenced to death. Rodney Legg in his book *Mysterious Dorset* says that the men were sentenced to death by being gibbeted, hung in chains to suffer a slow, agonising death, near the scene of their crime. Gibbeting was the usual punishment for highway robbery, but only after execution by hanging. The bodies would usually be covered in pitch and hung in gibbets as a warning to others not to offend.

The ghosts of Thomas Baker and his horse are said to appear with their cart on the anniversary of his death.

Above: Batcombe Church is associated with an amusing legend - that of John "Conjuror" Minterne, a local squire well versed in the dark arts. While out riding on the downs he remembered having left his book of spells open. Wishing to get back quickly, he spurred his horse and together they flew over the church, knocking one of the pinnacles to the ground.

Durdle Door [near Lulworth Cove]

Durdle Door must be one of the most photographed locations in the country. A natural arch eroded by the sea, it is made from Purbeck Limestone deposited in tropical fresh-water lagoons which teemed with life, including dinosaurs. It is a perfect focal point for some of the finest coastal scenery in Dorset.

Like its picturesque neighbour Worbarrow Bay, it was another favourite location for smugglers. As you enjoy the magnificent views from the coastal path, remember what its original purpose was; a means for the Riding Officers of the Revenue Service to patrol the coast looking out for smugglers. Naturally Durdle Door has seen its fair share of violence from those days. In June 1832 Lieutenant Thomas Edward Knight, Chief Coastguard Officer, was set upon by a gang of smugglers. He was viciously beaten and thrown off the cliff near Durdle Door. He was forty-two. Unlike Worbarrow, where legend says a smuggler was cruelly beaten to death, no ghostly apparitions accompany this story. Perhaps this tells us something about the sympathies of the people at the time. Most would not have regarded smuggling morally as a crime, whereas the Revenue were part of the system that kept many people in poverty.

Durdle Door does have its own legend however. In *Mysterious Dorset* Rodney Legg tells how the young maidservants from Lulworth Castle disappeared when the castle burned in 1929. They were never seen again and the story circulated that they had vanished from the cliffs near Durdle Door. He says he was sent a story that in the 1930s a sailor at anchor off Durdle Door had heard screaming from the shore one dark night. When he looked the figures of young girls gradually appeared, dancing in the waves. After a short while the figures faded and disappeared.

Durdle Door in the setting sun.

Shaftesbury

Like other Dorset towns and villages such as Cranborne and Bere Regis, Shaftesbury is a once bustling, administrative centre that has glided gracefully into the 21st century, delighting visitors and residents with its fascinating history and tranquil setting. There is something uniquely atmospheric about a place that once had grand buildings and witnessed events of national importance, but now has little to show except a picturesque charm.

Central to Shaftesbury's history is the abbey, of which there are few remains apart from stone foundations set in a pretty garden. The abbey was founded by Alfred the Great in AD 888, just after he had established the town as one of a number of fortified "burghs", designed as places of refuge for the population in time of Viking attack. Alfred had recently defeated the Danes and set about making sure that Wessex would not suffer years of warfare again.

The town and abbey prospered and in 979 something happened that was to secure wealth and prosperity for the abbey for the next 500 years. The body of King Edward the Martyr which had been discovered near Corfe Castle the year before, first buried in Wareham, was now transferred to Shaftesbury for permanent rest. Rumours of miracles began to grow up surrounding the body and Edward was canonised in 1001. Thus Shaftesbury became a centre for pilgrimage and visitors flocked to its holy shrine. As with such places today, visitors bring wealth and the abbey grew to be one of the richest in England, and the abbess to be a hugely powerful and influential figure. If you visit the abbey, stand on the path outside the walls and admire the extensive view over the Vale of Blackmore. All you can see once belonged to the abbey!

A further spur to the abbey's growth was royal patronage. It was, apparently, a favourite place of King Canute who died there in 1035. Catherine of Aragon once stayed there after coming to England to marry Prince Arthur.

There are a number of mysterious legends associated with the abbey. In 1971 a group of young people reportedly saw a figure of a young man dashing about the ruins at night. They claimed he would suddenly appear at one end of the abbey after apparently disappearing at the other end. After a while the figure vanished completely. Some have associated this with the ghost of King Edward. In 1931 a lead casket was unearthed in the grounds which contained the bones of a young man. The remains were carbon dated to Anglo-Saxon times. Could this have been the body of Edward the Martyr?

The main ghost of Shaftesbury Abbey is that of a monk who wanders the abbey grounds. It has been said that the monk is only visible from the knees up, reflecting the fact that the ground level is somewhat higher now than it used to be. The monk is often associated with another legend; that there is a haul of treasure buried somewhere in the grounds, hidden as a precaution by a monk who died of a heart attack before he could tell anyone where he had buried it. He must be a very tormented soul!

Right: The statue of King Alfred in the gardens of Shaftesbury Abbey. Alfred founded the abbey in 888 and made his daughter the first abbess.

Left: Only the foundations are left of the once rich Shaftesbury Abbey. At the far end is the shrine to King Edward "the Martyr" whose body now possibly rests with a Russian Orthodox church near Woking.

31

Barrows

Burial barrows have long been known as things of great antiquity. Thanks to modern dating techniques we now know that long barrows date back to the Neolithic or New Stone Age, more than 2500 BC, while round barrows were the work of Bronze Age peoples between about 2500 and 800 BC. Such mounds are found in large numbers dotted around the Dorset countryside, sometimes associated with more mysterious ceremonial structures, most famously at Knowlton where barrows lie scattered around a Neolithic henge monument with a ruined Norman church inside for good measure! Knowlton is thought to have been a major ceremonial centre like Stonehenge.

Almost all barrows have now been excavated - either scientifically or more simply pillaged by Victorian fortune hunters, but for hundreds of years these structures would have been part of the landscape for country people. Unsurprising that much folklore has grown up around them. A number of barrows have been credited with containing rich treasure, notably golden coffins. A very few barrows have indeed yielded valuable artefacts, some golden, probably the last resting places of Bronze Age chieftains.

Bottlebush Down near Sixpenny Handley has a number of round and long barrows and was clearly regarded as a special site for many hundreds of years. There have been sightings here of a spectral horseman clad in Bronze Age attire who disappears into a long barrow. The website "mysteriousbritain" claims there have been many witnesses, including respectable archaeologists.

On Bincombe Down in the parish of Whitcombe sits a barrow with a charming legend. It is said that if you put your ear to the top of the barrow at midday you will hear beautiful music. Rodney Legg in his book *Mysterious Dorset* claims to have tried this and not heard anything, speculating that perhaps the excavation of the barrow had been responsible for disturbing the musical spirits!

Peter Knight in his book *Ancient Stones of Dorset* tells of a strange happening at another barrow on Bincombe Hill. He says in the 1980s a woman noticed an orange glow around the barrow with "flames" shooting upwards. He believes this could be the result of earth energies at a site recognised by ancient people as special in some way. Similarly there is much folklore about ancient stones. Some are said to move, others the site of apparitions, while some have miraculous healing powers.

A more ghoulish legend is associated with the barrow at Trent near Sherborne in north Dorset. Near the barrow is a deep pool, so deep that it is claimed it is bottomless. The story goes that on a dark, stormy night a coach and horses veered off course and disappeared into the pit, never to be seen again. The sound of frightened horses and wailing passengers can sometimes be heard again on wild, windy nights. The pool has another legend: it is one of the places associated with Excalibur, King Arthur's magical sword, which was returned to the Lady of the Lake on his death. Although Dozmary Pool on Bodmin Moor has more popularly been associated with this mythical event, the pool at Trent also lays claim to it. Just a few miles away is Cadbury Castle, one of the most likely sites for Arthur's capital, Camelot.

The manor house at Trent is famously associated with one of the great adventures of English history, King Charles II's flight from defeat at the Battle of Worcester. Charles was disguised as a servant and had to stay well hidden in a village that was strongly anti-royalist. He allegedly grew very cross when the church bells were rung in mistaken celebration of his capture. He returned to the village a second time when the promise of a boat to the continent at Charmouth failed to materialise.

Left: Trent Barrow - yet another ancient site with Arthurian associations.
Below left: Trent church whose bells so angered King Charles II.

Below: Ackling Dyke, an old Roman road cutting across Bottlebush Down where the phantom Bronze Age horseman is said to ride. A number of barrows can be seen to the left of the road.

33

Corfe Castle [5 miles south of Wareham]

To many people the magnificent ruins at Corfe Castle are not particularly mysterious; they seem so familiar. In summer hundreds of tourists wander around and there is a party atmosphere. However, look past the holiday fun and you will see the remains of a mighty fortification, built both for protection and suppression in a violent age. For those interested in "horrible histories" Corfe Castle does not disappoint.

One of the most well-known events in the castle's history happened in AD 979, before the present stone structure had been built. It was here that, after a day's hunting, the young King Edward was murdered, probably on the orders of his step-mother who wanted her son Ethelred to be king. The deed shocked the nation, even in an age used to violence and treachery. Edward was later canonised and buried in Shaftesbury which became a place of pilgrimage. Edward's body was initially thrown down a well by his murderers and in their book *Haunted Dorset*, Chris Ellis and Andy Owens report that ghostly lights have been seen around the well, through the years and in modern times.

The Normans took over the stronghold of the Anglo-Saxons and over time built the stone castle we see today. It became a favourite lodging for King John who loved to hunt around here and also used it to store treasure. He once held 22 French noblemen here and starved them to death in the dungeons. Ellis and Owens say that people have heard strange moaning noises around where the dungeons used to be.

The most famous ghost of Corfe Castle is probably associated with the violent events that led to the castle's destruction in 1646. As with many of England's castles in these turbulent times, Corfe was the scene of a Civil War siege. Dorset was held by the forces of Parliament, but Sir John Bankes, the owner of Corfe Castle, was a staunch royalist. He died in 1644 but his widow, Lady Bankes, successfully organised the defence of the castle until the defences were breached in 1646 due to the treachery of one of the garrison. Many have since seen the ghost of a headless woman walking the battlements and the path leading up to the castle, possibly the woman who betrayed the castle to the Parliamentarians. The "Dark Dorset" website reports that she was seen by a man in 1967, drifting across the road in front of his car as he drove home late one night.

Corfe Castle has it all, a stunning setting, enigmatic ruins, tales of heroism and dastardly deeds, legends and ghost stories. It is fun to visit and wander around, but equally rewarding is to come early on a misty morning or as the sun is setting and climb the chalk ridge either side of the castle. You will be rewarded with an enchanting view of one of England's most spectacular and mysterious castles.

Above: Corfe Castle viewed from the chalk ridge to the east where the full extent of the castle can be appreciated. It must have been an awesome sight when complete.
Left: Looking out from the castle's fortifications.

Above: Athelhampton showing the original 15th century crenellated building and the 16th century West Wing.

Below: The Great Hall where the phantom duellists sometimes demonstrate their swordplay.

Athelhampton [Puddletown, 6 miles east of Dorchester]

Athelhampton is a quintessential English country manor house, grand yet homely architecture, rich, golden stone and beautifully manicured gardens bordering a river. Naturally it has a collection of ghosts and a history that goes back to Saxon times.

The Domesday book records the manor belonging to the Bishop of Salisbury, while before that it belonged to Aethelric. In old English "ham" means farm and "ton" an enclosure, so Athelhampton seems to have been a farm belonging to "Athel" or "Aethel". Some sources say that the manor may stand on the site of a palace of King Athelstan but the official guide does not mention this. The manor did not remain in Saxon hands for long after the conquest and it was the descendant of a Norman family, Sir William Martyn, who built Athelhampton in 1485, the year of the Battle of Bosworth Field and the beginning of the Tudor era. Sir William became Lord Mayor of London and obtained a licence to fortify the manor from Henry VII. The need to obtain the king's permission to do this dated back to a time when noblemen lived in fortified castles which could be used as strongholds in uprisings against the king. In the age of gunpowder and ever improving artillery a few crenellations on a manor house were not going to pose a threat to national security! The Great Hall dates from this time and the West Wing was built in the early 16th century. Over the following centuries the house was added to further and it has remained in private hands for over 500 years.

Athelhampton has a reputation as one of the most haunted houses in England. Unusually its most famous ghost is not of a human but an ape. An ape appears in the coat of arms of the Martyn family who owned the hall in the 16th century. The last of this family owned a pet ape and in 1595 when the last lord of the manor died it appears the ape was somehow trapped in a secret staircase and starved to death. Some say he was searching for a new master but could only find four daughters. Since then he has been heard scratching and trying desperately to get out of his prison.

In the wine cellar a phantom cooper is sometimes heard tapping at barrels and in the Great Hall ghostly duellists have been witnessed clashing swords until one is wounded and they disappear. The protagonists seem to date from the Civil War when the house was loyal to the Royalist cause. No self-respecting medieval manor would be complete without the ghost of a grey or headless lady; Athelhampton has the former spectre. The Grey Lady glides through walls between the East Wing and the State and Yellow bedrooms. On one occasion an employee asked a lady to leave who she had come across sitting sometime after the house had closed for the night. The lady rose and disappeared through the wall!

Sandford Orcas [3 miles north of Sherborne]

In the tiny village of Sandford Orcas near Sherborne is a delightful little Tudor manor house built of exquisite Ham Hill Stone. The Lower Jurassic oceans in this part of the world generally produced sandstones and clays, but at some stage the environment changed and a gorgeous, rich yellow limestone was deposited. Many fine buildings have been constructed from this excellent stone.

At first glance it is difficult to imagine a more beautiful place to live. However, there are many who would not be tempted to spend a night in this idyllic spot, for the manor is reputed to be the most haunted house in England. You will find accounts of its legion of ghosts in many books and websites. But Sandford Orcas should perhaps be famous for another reason; it is as a testament to our willingness and indeed ambition to believe in the supernatural. You will find no mention of the manor in JS Udal's definitive book on Dorset folklore, surprising when it details many less spectacular ghost stories. The presence of ghosts has been firmly denied by previous owners and the present owner is likewise dismissive of the hauntings.

It seems the spooky stories may have been started by an eccentric tenant of the manor, Colonel Francis Claridge, who lived in the house in the 1960s. The Colonel told of countless ghostly encounters, welcomed the press and anybody who would listen to his increasingly macabre stories of the history of the manor. Even to the most ardent believer in the supernatural the stories must have begun to look like pure fantasy, with every ghostly stereotype included somewhere.

In their recent book, *Haunted Dorset,* Chris Ellis and Andy Owens make the point that many more people claim to have also witnessed hauntings at Sandford Orcas, including domestic staff and visitors to the manor. Have some of these people been prompted to report seemingly strange goings on by stories they may have heard in the press or are they genuinely unexplained events? Perhaps it is like UFO sightings; once someone claims to have seen a UFO at a certain location it's amazing how many more sightings there subsequently are.

However, it seems the Colonel, whose motives remain unclear, has done enough to ensure that Sandford Orcas still appears in books and on websites as a genuine, and indeed typical, haunted English manor house. Significantly, serious paranormal investigators have stayed at the manor and reported nothing unusual. Perhaps that adds to the mystery of other sites; maybe it somehow reinforces the credibility of other, less flamboyant ghostly legends?

Beautiful Sandford Orcas manor in the village of the same name a few miles north of Sherborne. The manor was built in the early 16th century from local Ham Hill Stone, a rich, mellow limestone from the Jurassic.

A Saxon manor probably once existed here and after the conquest the estate was given to a Norman called Orescuilz, from which the name Orcas derives. The Medleycott family have owned the house since the middle of the 18th century.

Bibliography and Further Reading

Mysterious Dorset by Rodney Legg [Dorset Publishing Company]
A very comprehensive book, mostly about ghosts but also including legends, customs and superstitions.

Legends by Jeremy Harte [Dovecote Press, Discover Dorset series]
Legends brought to life as interesting stories.

Haunted Dorset by Chris Ellis and Andy Owens [S. B. Publications]
A good guide to the more well known ghost stories.

Ghosts of Dorset by Peter Underwood [Bossiney]
Lots of information and new stories from one of the country's leading writers on ghosts.

Dorsetshire Folk-Lore by John Symonds Udal [Dorset Books]
The definitive guide to Dorset's folklore.

Useful websites:

www.darkdorset.co.uk
Lots of articles and a fun site, plus links to many other good websites.

www.paranormaldatabase.com
A very comprehensive nationwide site.

www.themodernantiquarian.com
A very useful database.

www.mysteriousbritain.co.uk
Another useful nationwide database.

www.stoneseeker.net
A site about ancient mysteries by Dorset's own expert, Peter Knight.